For all my dear loved ones,
past and present.

© Rayner Tapia, 2024

All rights reserved. No part of this book may be reproduced or utilised in any form or by any means, electronic or mechanical, including photocopying, recording, or by any information storage and retrieval system, without permission in writing from the author.

First published in 2024
Written by Rayner Tapia
Illustrated by Marian Marinov
Book design by Bryony van der Merwe

ISBN: 978-1-915495-39-6 (hardcover)

Heartstone House Ltd
75 Greenwood Road
Sheffield, S35 3GU
info@heart-stone-house.co.uk

DISCLAIMER: The *Harry the Hedgehog* series is a work of fiction intended for children. Any resemblance to real persons, living or deceased, is purely coincidental. The characters, events, and settings in this book are products of the author's imagination and are not meant to represent any real individuals, organisations, or places.

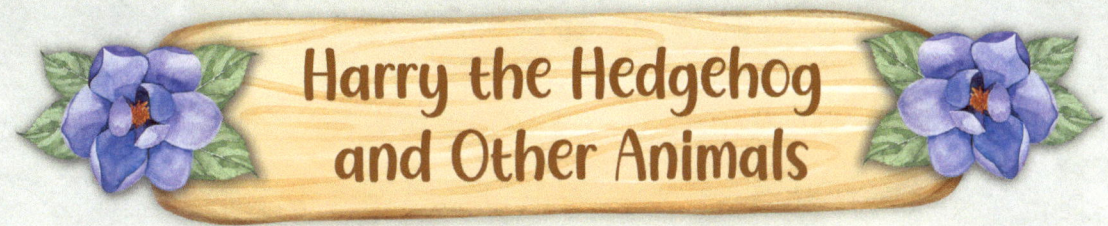

Harry the Hedgehog and Other Animals

Harry the Hedgehog
Meets Danny the Dog

Written by
Rayner Tapia

Illustrated by Marian Marinov

Once upon a time, a hedgehog named Harry lived in a cosy burrow in the corner of a green garden.

Harry was a cheerful little
fellow, always

sniffing out new adventures,

and making friends.

He had a spiky coat that he was **very proud of**

and tiny paws that were perfect for **scampering about.**

Curious and a little cautious, Harry the hedgehog followed the noise until he *reached a small school.*

There, he saw a big, *friendly-looking brown dog* with floppy ears and a *wagging tail.*

"Hello!" called Harry the Hedgehog from the safety of a bush. *"Who are you?"*

Danny the Dog smiled.
"Well, it's nice to meet you, Harry!
What brings you here?"

"I wanted to see who was barking,"
Harry the Hedgehog admitted.
"What are you doing?"

"I was playing fetch with my human friend," Danny the Dog explained. "It's a game where they throw a stick, and I bring it back. Do you want to play?"

Harry's eyes sparkled with excitement.
"That sounds like fun! But I'm not very good at fetching sticks."

"That's okay," Danny the Dog said kindly. "We can find something else to play together."

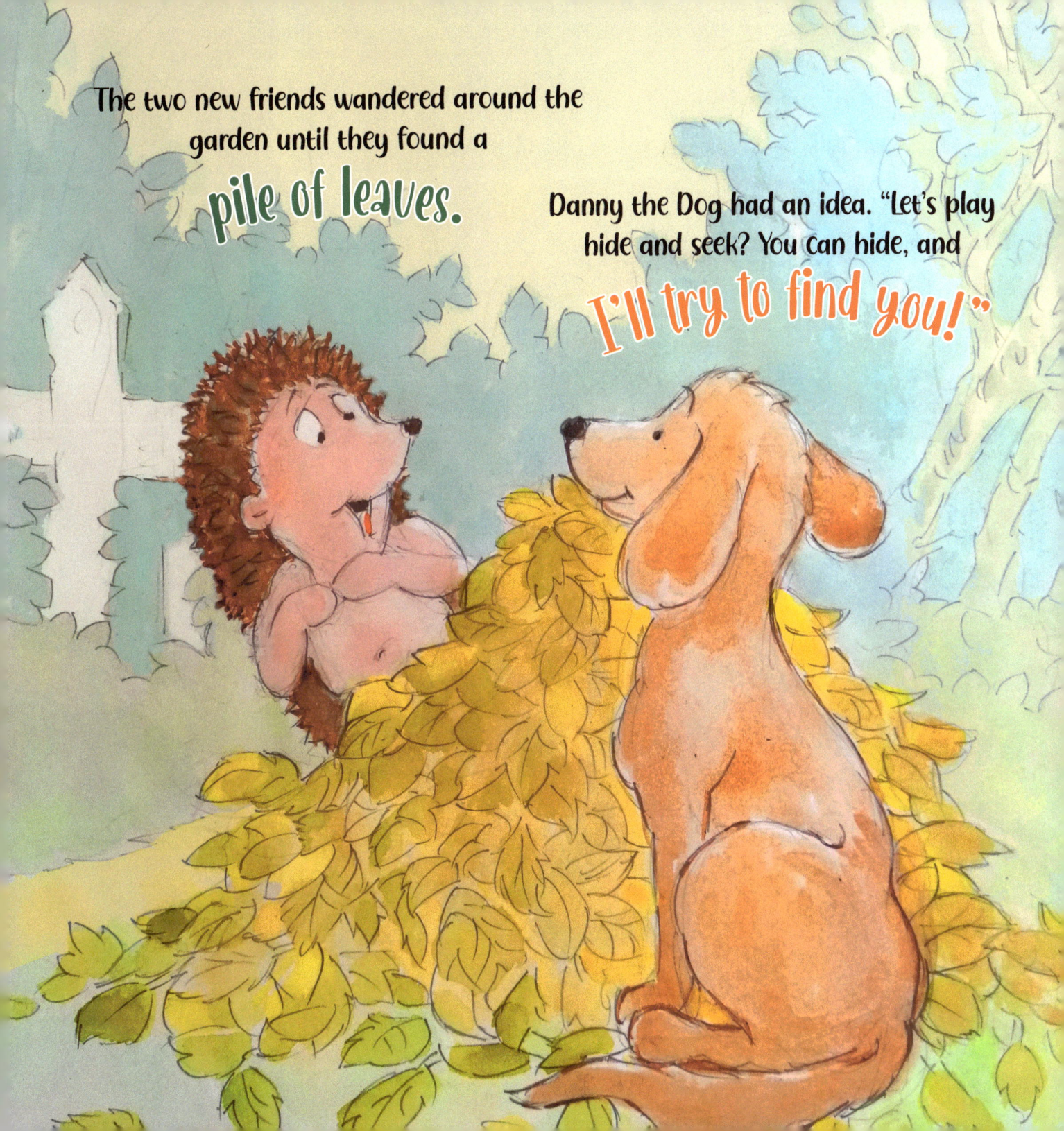

The two new friends wandered around the garden until they found a **pile of leaves.**

Danny the Dog had an idea. "Let's play hide and seek? You can hide, and *I'll try to find you!*"

Harry the Hedgehog loved this idea.
He quickly scurried under a big pile of leaves,
his spiky back blending perfectly.
"Ready!" he called out.

Danny the Dog sniffed around, using his nose to search. It didn't take long for him to find the

cleverly hidden hedgehog.

"Found you!"

Danny the Dog barked happily, his tail wagging.

Harry the Hedgehog popped out of the leaves, laughing. "You're really good at this!"

"Thanks," said Danny the Dog. "Shall I hide this time?"

"Yes!" Harry the Hedgehog, said eagerly. "I want to try to find you."

Danny found a big tree and crouched behind it.
"Ready!" he called.

Harry the Hedgehog used his keen sense of smell to track Danny the Dog. It was tricky, but soon enough, he found Danny.

"Found you!" Harry cheered.

The two friends played and laughed all morning with big smiles and happy hearts, reminding each other that the best part of the game is

the joy of being together.

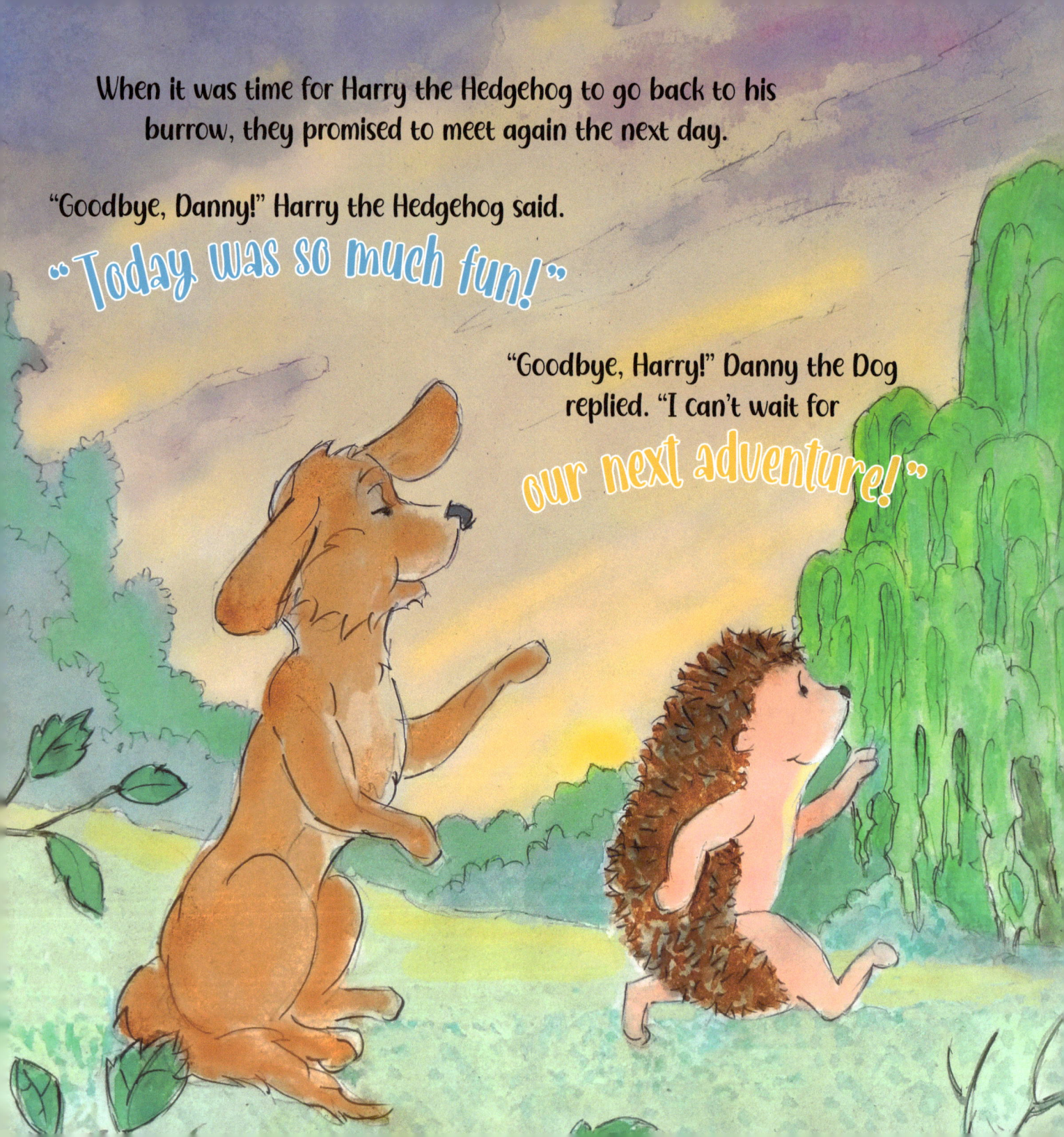

When it was time for Harry the Hedgehog to go back to his burrow, they promised to meet again the next day.

"Goodbye, Danny!" Harry the Hedgehog said. "Today was so much fun!"

"Goodbye, Harry!" Danny the Dog replied. "I can't wait for our next adventure!"

And so, Harry the Hedgehog and Danny the Dog became the best of friends, always eager for the next sunny day when they could play together.

The garden was never the same and was always filled *with their laughter and joy.*

The End.

About the Author

Rayner Tapia is one of the NABE Pinnacle Book Achievement winners; The Dream Catcher won the 2012 NABE for Best Juvenile Fiction Books. NABE winner 2016 Best Sci-fiction book and honorary award for Literature, Florida. Rayner Tapia lives in London with her family. She is an IT trainer/teacher for children and adults. She recently (2019) passed English with Distinction, CPD, 2-4 Teaching Literacy in Schools. She is a published author and entrepreneur. Rayner has worked in banking, and has taught IT and English.

www.ingramcontent.com/pod-product-compliance
Lightning Source LLC
Chambersburg PA
CBHW041507220426
43661CB00017B/1271